# Beetles
## Around the World

Written by Sally Morgan

## Contents

**Collins**

# Beetles

Beetles are incredible insects. They are found everywhere, from tropical jungles to mountain tops. Despite their tiny size, beetles achieve amazing physical feats.

head

legs

body

wing

# Largest beetles

Titan beetles are giants compared with other beetles. They look terrifying, but they eat plants!

A titan beetle is the length of your hand.

**Fact**

Their powerful jaws can snap a twig.

5

# Fastest beetles

Tiger beetles cannot fly, but they scuttle quickly on six legs. This aggressive hunter chases after its prey. When the prey is captured, it is ripped apart and eaten.

# Jumping beetles

Click beetles jump without using their legs!
When scared, click beetles lie on their backs and
pretend to be dead. With a click, they
hurl themselves into the air to escape.
They spin, land on the ground
and scuttle away.

# Brightest beetles

Jewel beetles are shiny and bright. Some look like gold. Light reflects off their shiny bodies to help them blend into their surroundings.

# Defensive beetles

Some beetles protect themselves
with weapons. These beetles
squirt a jet of burning liquid
at attackers.

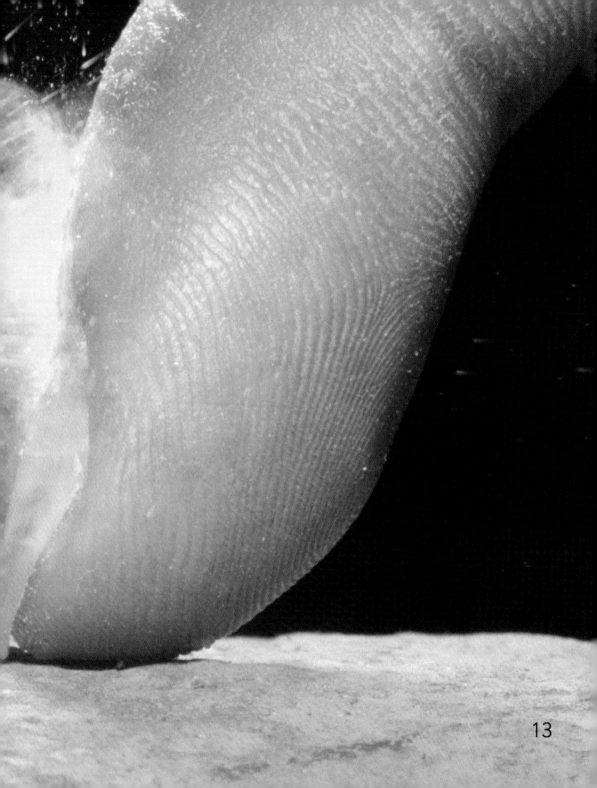

# Strangest beetles

These beetles have very long necks! What kind of animal do you think they look like?

**Fact**

Male beetles
use their necks
to fight.

15

# Strongest beetles

Male Hercules beetles are
incredibly strong.
They burrow in deep
leaves in forests.

horn-like pincers for fighting

claws for burrowing

# Deadly beetles

Arrow poison beetles live in the desert. Adults are harmless, but the immature beetles, called grubs, contain a harmful poison. The grubs get the poison from the plants they eat.

grub

**Fact**

The San people smear their arrow tips with poison from these beetles when they go hunting.

Next time you see a beetle, stop and take a look.
They may be small, but they are amazing creatures.

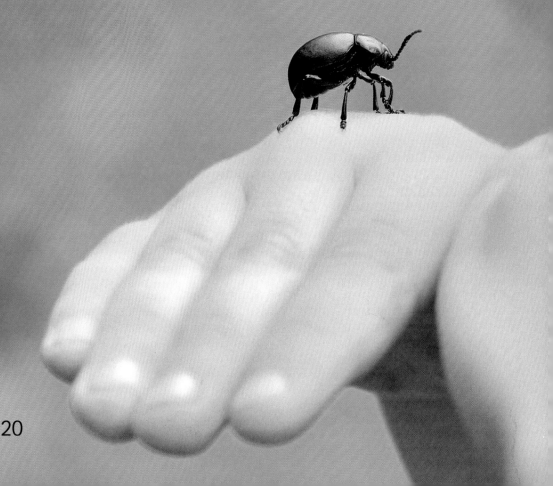

# The beetles

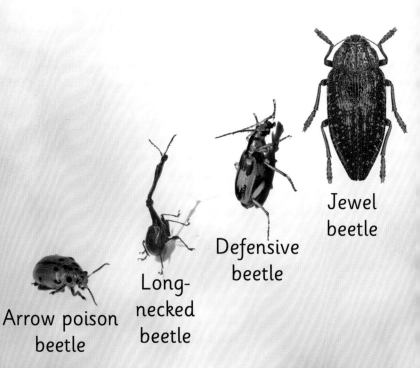

Jewel
beetle

Defensive
beetle

Long-
necked
beetle

Arrow poison
beetle

Click
beetle

Ladybird

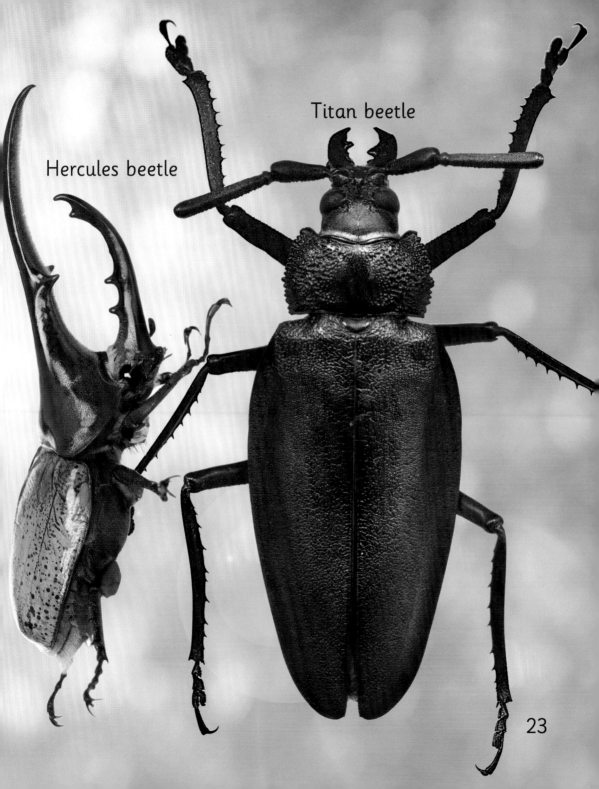

Hercules beetle

Titan beetle

23

# ❧ After reading ❧

**Letters and Sounds:** Phase 5

**Word count:** 315

**Focus phonemes:** /igh/ y ie /ee/ y e /w/ wh /v/ ve /l/ le / ch/ t /ai/ a/j/ g ge /f/ ph /z/ se

**Common exception words:** of, to, the, into, are, were, their, people

**Curriculum links:** Science: Animals, including humans

**National Curriculum learning objectives:** Spoken language: articulate and justify answers, arguments and opinions; Reading/Word reading: apply phonic knowledge and skills as the route to decode words, read accurately by blending sounds in unfamiliar words containing GPCs that have been taught, read other words of more than one syllable that contain taught GPCs, read aloud accurately books that are consistent with their developing phonic knowledge; Reading/Comprehension: understand both the books they can already read accurately and fluently ... by: drawing on what they already know or on background information and vocabulary provided by the teacher

## Developing fluency

- Your child may enjoy hearing you read the book. Model reading with lots of expression.
- You may wish to take turns to read a page.

## Phonic practice

- Look at the word **incredibly** on page 16. Explain that in this word the 'y' grapheme is pronounced /ee/. Practise sounding out each syllable 'chunk' and blending them together.
  in/cred/i/bly
- Then read each chunk to read the whole word.
- Now do the same for the following words:
  - ○ strangest ('ge' is pronounced /j/)
  - ○ giants ('g' is pronounced /j/)

## Extending vocabulary

- Talk about what an adjective is. (*a describing word*)